W9-BQT-249

recognize

recognize

Poems by Kevin Powell

Published for Harlem River Press by:
Writers and Readers Publishing, Inc.
P.O. Box 461, Village Station
New York, New York 10014

Copyright © 1995 by Kevin Powell

Cover Photograph: Carl Posey
Cover Design: Terrie Dunkelberger
Book Design: Terrie Dunkelberger

This book is sold subject to the condition that it shall not, by way of trade or otherwise, be lent, re-sold, hired out, or otherwise circulated without the publisher's prior consent in any form of binding or cover than that in which it is published and without a similar condition being imposed on the subsequent purchaser.

All rights reserved. No part of this publication may be reproduced, stored in a retrieval system, or transmitted, in any form or by any means, electronic, mechanical, photocopying, recording or otherwise, without the prior permission of the Publisher.

ISBN: 0-86316-324-6

0 9 8 7 6 5 4 3 2 1

Manufactured in the United States of America

Some of the poems in this book previously appeared in *Catalyst*, *In The Tradition: An Anthology of Young Black Writers*, *American Idealism Rag*, *Obsidian II*, *Vibe*, *The Source*, *Aloud: Voices from the Nuyorican Poets Cafe*, *New Word*, *Young Tongues*, *Take Five*, *Sing*, *Mixed Media*, on MTV, and at the High Museum of Art (Atlanta, Ga.).

This book is dedicated to Morris Staton II (MSII):
caged birds will wreck shop...

Contents

Acknowledgments

Special thanks to Glenn Thompson and Writers and Readers Publishing, Deborah Dyson, Beth Smith, *Vibe*, MTV, Bob Holman, Miguel Algarin, The Nuyorican Poets Cafe, my agent Sarah Lazin, Pearl Cleage, Catherine Smith Jones and family, Jabari & Liana Asim, Ira Jones, Andrea Wren, Radcliffe Bailey, Lisa Teasley, Michael Datcher, Tracy Carness, Sonia Sanchez, Nelson George, Charlie Braxton, Danyel Smith, Carl Posey, Michelle T. Clinton, The National Black Arts Festival, Robin Wheeler, Major Jackson and The Painted Bride Art Center, Jonathan Van Meter, Diane Cardwell, all the contributors to *In The Tradition*, Jim Roberts, Shirley Mae Powell (thanks for the push, always!), the entire Bur(r)ison Family, all the colleges and universities where I've read and lectured, and Ni'Cole (I love you & thank you for the title).

To our everlasting shame and glory what we may recognize first is something we are not.

—John Edgar Wideman

autobiographical notes

I was born twenty-eight years ago in Jersey City, NJ, the only child of a single mother. It was that reality and the high drama of inner city life that shaped who I am today. I was an inquisitive and ambitious child: I loved school, nearly overdosed on television, and swore that one day I would play baseball for the New York Yankees.

Because the ghetto affords little in the way of luxury, my imagination had to make up for whatever material resources we didn't have. So I dreamed a lot: about mystical, faraway places; about life in a bigger home (we never lived in a house) with a bigger family with bigger dinners; about the lives of other people. In spite of my excellent grades and the push of my mother ("you gonna be a lawyer"), however, my "real life" seemed like it would never reach beyond the narrow spaces we occupied in Jersey City.

But that changed when I was 12 or 13. My mother took me to the Greenville Public Library every other week or so and on a particular Saturday I, rather than venturing toward the sports section as I normally did, stumbled into the fiction section. There I crossed the name "Ernest Hemingway" and was fascinated by the title of his book: *For Whom The Bell Tolls*. Yeah, I thought, who does it toll for if it ain't tollin' for me?

I scooped the book up and read it from cover to cover even though I lost myself in the Spanish words and the details of the Spanish Civil War. Hemingway had taken me somewhere, away from the stiff boundaries of my life. Who was this Hemingway guy anyway? I looked up his life story and was captivated: he traveled the world, dined in exotic places, he lived. Well damn, if this is what a writer does, I thought, then that is what I want to be.

Over the next few years my mind ran wild with urban tales of mayhem and adventure. I absorbed Shakespeare and Dickens and became particularly fond of Edgar Allan Poe's ghoulish narratives. I adapted my short story style to his and penned ghettocentric murder mysteries. I felt empowered.

High school was an uneventful time for me. I attended three different schools, finally landing at Henry Snyder High School, reportedly one of the worst in the state. It was there that I met Mrs. Lillian Williams, my 12th grade English teacher, who drilled into my head the importance of the written word. With her encouragement I entered two essay contests — one a city-wide competition — and won both.

When I graduated I was presented with a special writing award in recognition of my achievements and I was off to college to study, initially, computers. But that changed the moment I hit the campus of Rutgers University. Charged by the anti-apartheid movement gripping colleges and universities nationwide, I found my 18-year-old mind swept up into the politics of change. And college did change me. My heretofore theoretical interests in the world now became practical: I joined every black organization in sight and truly believed a revolution could be launched from our student offices. And my need to express my feelings was re-ignited. So I joined the black student weekly, the *Black Voice/Carta Boricua* newspaper, and became one of its leading reporters (I gainfully studied the history of Woodward and Bernstein and swore I too would become a top-notch investigative reporter). At age 20 I commuted part-time to New York City to work as a cub reporter for the now-defunct *Black American* newspaper. I covered the Michael Griffith murder in Howard Beach and found myself staring at Mayor Ed Koch at City Hall press conferences. Two years later my political activities got me kicked out of college and I found myself in Newark, NJ, struggling to make ends meet and writing very bad poetry to heal myself.

The last few years have indeed been an odyssey: I wound up on MTV as a cast member of a very popular show called "The Real World," I co-edited (with Ras Baraka) *In The Tradition: An Anthology of Young Black Writers*, and I've been published in numerous newspapers, magazines, and journals including *Vibe* magazine where I'm presently a staff writer.

To say that I am lucky to be doing what I love to do and getting paid for it would be an understatement. I have no delusions that all of this could end tomorrow and I'd be back teaching writing to high school kids and writing publicity BIOS for record companies.

But I don't plan for that to happen. Writing is my life. In many ways it has saved my life. The poems and essays, particularly, have served as a mirror for me to reflect upon my inner conflicts, my victories, my losses. I think every artist is obligated to dig deep within him- or herself if he or she intends on being true *and* real. I don't think my work has been especially spectacular but I've never been afraid to expose my thoughts, my views, and, in essence, me, to this thing we call life.

For sure, writing is an evolutionary process. There are things I wrote three and four years ago which I shudder to think came from my pen. On the other hand, there are things I want to write badly which have been elusive. I write not only about my personal experiences but also about larger themes which affect this society. That is, from my specific experiences come an informed opinion about America and the world.

Indeed, as a black writer I find it absolutely necessary to write from the perspective of an African American. That is what I am and that knowledge has given me a particular type of lens with which to view the world. Historically, blackfolks have been written out of the realities of this nation and even where we have made tremendous contributions — be it in politics, culture, sports, or the intellectual realm — our contributions have either been poorly documented or not at all.

I don't pretend to know everything. I do know, however, that there is something grotesquely wrong with a society where millions of people face daily political, cultural, spiritual, psychological, and economic oppression by virtue of their skin complexion. That said, much of my work deals in some manner with the cancer we call racism as well as the all-important identity questions which accompany it.

I have many fears: I fear failure (my standards are high as hell); I fear unimaginative people; I fear cowards; and I fear myself whenever I become afraid to operate to my fullest potential. Writing is perhaps the most courageous thing I've ever done. To be able to state my opinions on a piece of paper then have those thoughts published will always amaze me. Never in my wildest dreams did I think my words would matter to anyone save a school teacher or a girlfriend.

It is writing that has fulfilled some of my childhood dreams and made it possible for me to travel, to speak, to touch and feel other human beings. I once asked an older writer for advice and he said I should just let the world be my walkman. I agree. We are so lost in the technological creations of humankind that we've misplaced the ability to feel and read and understand each other. I want my writing to open up minds, feed souls, bridge gaps, provoke heated exchanges; I want my writing to breathe and live forever. Why else would I do this if not to transform myself and the world in some small way?

for aunt cathy

life ain't never been promised to nobody
that's what grandma lottie used to say
and you
her youngest daughter
and youngest of six children
snuck into the city
on a greyhound bus
with my mother
and scraped the side of a boarding house for good luck
as your life stretched beyond
the wooden shacks
and cotton fields
and the sandy school room floors of south carolina

and you were alive
at last
free
in a city
away from the
comforting stench of down south
and in the big city
with its
musty underarm
and gasoline breath

and you took all ten years of your schoolin'
and applied for a job as a factory worker
on the assembly line
and you assembled parts

and the parts assembled you into
the permanence of minimum wages
and time clocks
and bosses who thought a black woman
was supposed to like work
hell, y'all had been conditioned to be oxes
they figured

and when you wasn't producing like an ox
their tucked-in pot bellies would ask:
why you moving so slow cathy?
and on the inside you licked your tongue
at them the way you used to do
when my mother and my aunt birdie yelled at you
and your heart tightened around your waist
and you ate what your feet could produce
for eight hours a day
40 hours a week
with
one 15 minute break a day
if you was doing your job

and you needed something else
to keep your tears from spitting out
thoughts and words that would send you
back down south
in a fit of fear
and you met him
and he was fine

for aunt cathy ....

that man
and you liked him
and he liked you
and like became love
to you
and like became lust
for him
and he and you
exploded into anthony
my cousin anthony
one april day in 1966
and now you had a shield
to hold against the world
you had a world to shield you against
the heartaches of him
the foot aches of work
and the headaches
of city life

and you raised anthony
the best way you knew how
just like my mother raised me
and anthony grew and i grew
with our frustrated imaginations
to resent each other
to hate you, our mothers
to despise our very existences
in that tiny
cramped three-room apartment

two mothers and two sons
in a three-room apartment
held together
by welfare
food stamps
and the roaches
who always found their way
into our food
no matter how thick
the layers of aluminum foil

and that thirsty, tingling sensation
would often reappear
crawling between your toes
up your legs
across your thighs
teasing your crotch
but it couldn't get any further
that's nasty,
you thought,
some man between my legs
again
so you stuffed your womb
with the world of anthony
because your spirit
was tired of being probed
by social workers, mailmen, and would-be husbands
for having an illegitimate son

and in spite of reality
burning down every hope we had
we managed to spread out
to a better part of the ghetto
and we even had separate apartments now
but you and my mother
always was in the same building because
my mother was the mean one
who scoffed at the world
with her angry eyes
and you was the nice one
who wanted to be like my mother
but you couldn't
so you followed my mother
everywhere
because at least you'd be safe
from yourself

and when we finally moved out of the ghetto
around white folks
you felt good
we was movin' up
and flying like birds released from their mother's grip for
the first time
and we was happy to be around
white folks
and didn't mind being called niggas
because at least we was good niggas

and me and anthony
knocked off the weight of
that restless city
that dirty city
and we left:
me to college
anthony to the navy
leaving you and my mother
grazing in the pastures of mid-life

and my mother was happy to be free of a man-child
but you was sad
because anthony had been your reason to live
your reason to work
your reason to exist
and now his departure meant your death
and you were dying
a slow death
dancing with mid-life and dying a muted death
the years of working were gone
the years of sharing were gone
the years of being were gone
and the woman inside of your crouching body
died one may day in 1988 when grandma lottie was
buried
and as we wiped the tears from our eyes
no one noticed you sinking through the church pew
through the floor
into the earth to join grandma lottie

and even though anthony was there at the funeral
he left again
back to the navy
back to japan
to some strange place
that was not him
because he hated himself
and he hated you
for being him
and he nailed shut
the door
on your life

and no one noticed you drowning in your pain
until you began having conversations with yourself
and tellin' everyone how you was hearing things
and seeing movies on your living room wall
how you was the star in those movies

and even my mother
with her superstitious ways
could not believe
that you were a victim of roots and magic spells

and my mother and aunt birdie did it;
they tricked you with a meal and had you
straight-jacketed
and they didn't tell me

but i found out and i found you
and i leaped inside your body
and begged you to wake up
i swam inside your dried up tears
and turned back the currents
to your childhood
to your adolescence
to your early adulthood
to anthony
to anthony's father
to my mother and aunt birdie and grandma lottie
and i cried between the lines of your history

and you told me you were not crazy
and i said i know
and you told me you could not understand
why my mother and aunt birdie had put you there
and i said i know
and you told me how they drugged you
how they called you by a number
how they monitored your phone calls
and i knew that you had become a prisoner of your
worst fears
                    of your own death

and i looked at you and i didn't see you
instead i saw an old black woman
inside your 45-year-old body

and i wanted to rush to you and shake your youth
out of that impostor

but it was you...

and now i understand those sounds you heard
and those movies you saw on your walls
you are not crazy
it took me a long time
but i understand
anthony knows what you've been through
but he doesn't know you
i know you
my mother and aunt birdie know what you've been
through
but they don't know you
i know you

i carry you with me everyday
i see you when i see that black woman
lying on the ground with a mcdonald's cup in her hand
at 34th street
i see you and i say
"here cathy,
this is all i got"
and i drop a tear into your cup
and curse myself and my mother and aunt birdie
and anthony and anthony's father
and i kiss you with a prayer

...........for aunt cathy

because now i understand
why black bodies sag the way they do
and why black hearts don't birth emotions anymore

Mental Terrorism

i wonder what wright and baldwin
    and all the other soothsayers
would say
if they could witness
the after effects
of the calculated explosion
    of 5 billion inhuman minds?

funny
    how things
        have gotten to this

vacant hearts have taken each other hostage
    and stumble forward
heading no where in particular
    doing nothing in particular
        looking for mr. or mrs. goodbar

the hero of the day:
    nelson mandela
yebo!
let's name a candy bar after him
    name it the freedom bar
rich
chocolate-
flavored
crunch
    that chips a tooth on every second byte

and if someone fucks with you or me
it converts into a semi-automatic ninja fighter
complete with copies of *the art of war*,
the anarchist cookbook,
and the holy bible

(of course
if you forget to freeze the bar
it will be quite ineffective as a means of
deterrence)

nel son man de la
will you free me please?
i've never met god
but
you sure are close
we love you mr. mandela
what is love anyway?
my mother and i
have never hugged
have never kissed
have never said
"i love you"
call me a stupefied stoic
however
the world's bloody palms
have yet to clutch my face
in pity

what is it to be locked away
in the imagination of kidnappers—
an unwanted and unappreciated spoil of war?

"underdog!
oh where oh where can my underdog be?"
bart simpson and arsenio hall
in that order
are the only two friends i have left
they will soon become bigger
than all the gods
in ancient africa
and forget that humankind exists day to day

can i cry in living color?
from buckwheat to the homeboy shopping network
will the negro ever learn the concept
of self-respect?
edutainment is the key
flip a switch
and rap a lyric
around a little kid's brain
call it
video music box
and yo! mtv raps
the music of a rebellious generation
generating truth from beneath the rubbish
of integrated nightmares

rhyth mic american po e try
you hear it
and you think of me
trapped in a concrete box
begging to be released
so that i can be told a thousand and one times
"well, you have a nice resume but..."
how many butts can one man have anyway?
and some of you have the nerve to condemn the
homeless!
all i want is the opportunity to have an opportunity
where does one run to when *stuck*
in the promised land?

how about central park?
the beast is smilin'
'cuz he went wildin'
in the dark
(Black folks never heard of the word "wildin'"
until 1989)
total recall is only a movie
coerced confessions
are revisited from scottsboro

(central park, too, deserves a song)

the sperm don't match
hoover's boys said that

i guess
somebody's gotta pay
for purity's guilt

only if malcolm had lived
only if martin had lived
only if the dead kennedys would rise
one eye on the prize
the other on the bush-man
flip-flopping like a misplaced fish on the beach
creating political vision
without political backbone

don't touch that flag!
it's live campaign ammunition

N-E-A stands for
Nazism Entering America
via congressional doors
2 bad and 2 live
for the average citizen who hasn't read
machiavelli
or tricky dicky nixon's lips

censoring is moral mccarthyism
and the '90s version of the lynch mob

big brother is watching you
watching me

i can't stop writing
in spite of my fears
who cares?

it's gettin'
it's gettin'
it's gettin' kinda hectic
but i've got the power to break out of this cage
at any moment...

beyond love spell number u..

i stare into a mirror:
my reflection slits its lips on a broken bottle.
tears are a narcissistic theme
landing somewhere between a dust trap
and your celestial remedies

our cat is a purring sphinx,
his eyes face the world at an evil angle
blood lines his water bowl
have we fed him lately?

note the spot where you mashed a fly
a triumph over nature!
however, my soul remains in an amorphous flux;
it rolls into a lint ball,
bouncing erratically through the bars in the window

Genius Child

for Langston Hughes

simple ain't it?
the words flow
like a river
winding
your smile

a thumb snaps
an eighth note
bebop!
a horn's lips curl
at a girl
in a red dress

you, too, fragment
a dark vein
it sings
it sags
like a blues bag
weighing dreams
on lenox avenue

kp

i spit into a glass
look, in the bubbles,
god is hand-checking
michael jordan

kp

'nuff respect
to the 'hood
that's got its own
mama's fried chicken shack

kp

save the earth!
unwrap a teardrop:
it needs to breathe sometimes

kp

don't hate them because
they are beautiful;
hate them because
they value dirt naps

kp

death flew into harlem
on a doo-rag
who told langston
he could hang himself
with a syllable?

altar for four

I.

four little girls

bombed for equal rights
a prayer yes yes say a prayer, brother
for the forgotten
we
shall
overcome
our overcomes and our overcames

DEAD

four little black girls

bodies greased, pressed and folded against the church pews
their heads
like halos
glow beneath the lord's window
no, sister
that window is not there anymore
it exploded on four little girls
the way that water hose broke old mister young's back

oh people, can you hear me?
what do we want?
freedom!
when do we want it?
now!
thirty years and counting
been countin' for thirty years now
done run out of toes and fingers to count on

II.

john coltrane
where have you gone?
we can still feel your sax dragging its tongue
along the carpet they call alabama
sweet sweet alabama
land of the cotton
why are those four little black girls
still bleeding in your belly?

III.

brothas and sistas, hah!
i'm here ta tell ya, hah!
that the laaawd don't like ugly, no! lawd don't like no ugliness
are y'all wid me?
i said are y'all wid me now?
these little girls ain't done nothin' to noooo-body
i said noooo-body
and for that they dead lawd
look at them sweet jeee-sus!
ain't got no toes left, hah!
ain't got no fingers left, hah!
can't count the time no more lawd, hah!
time done stop lawd, hah!
i said time done stop, hah!
what we gonna do lawd?
we gonna pick some flowers, hah!
and bury our future, hah!
and we gonna build a new house lawd
and we gonna paint it blue lawd
i said we gonna paint it blue, hah!
so we can feel that old-time spirit a-goin', hah!
feeel it! thank ya jesus!
feeel it! thank ya jesus!

IV.

at 16th and 6th they say it's
 not a home anymore
they say all the homes have been torn down
 that blackfolks don't live here anymore
just dusty flesh and charcoal bones
 with steam-iron memories
of this march or that song
they say
 the railroad tracks have moved
that just because you can cross 'em now
don't mean you gotta new home
you still gotta pack a gun
still gotta poke it into the sky like this:
bang!
they say:
 we're not bitter
 just hungry
 need some nourishment
 and some time
 and some homes
 and some freedom...

love/a many splintered thing

for Karla P.

i have this need to feel you
make love out of the sweat
itching our palms give
you to your mother so that she
can give birth to you create an
ocean where love sleeps peacefully
eat out of the same bed we flesh
orgasms scream where cobwebs
imprison courage cry   where
your tears gripped my shoulders wrap
my tongue around your waist and
lick the rhythms of your walk
talk until a beat hits me where
it hits me where it hits me
in the space   where my heart
used to be   you know it's
blank now   dark   black no
commercials open land
waiting to be folded and smoothed
out like the note i slipped you yesterday
that said you are me am you we are
do not be afraid i want to
help you help me   love a
many splintered thing i felt
yes   his tongue   slit my heart
as it parted your mouth
and i wanted to die   yeah
rope myself with my naiveté

drink reflection: share a walk on
lenox avenue with a friend who
gets high on pain two many times
we step on our eyelids and miss
the chance to l(i)ove the chance
to slide open a cloud with a kiss
when will trust not be for sale a
gun between the thighs a middle
finger aimed at the hungry a wish
stuffed inside two bodies crawling
on their tails scraping the bottom
of a dream

Reality Check

for Kurt Cobain (1967-1994)

i hate myself and want to die
i can hear you saying that now
the words like gunshots blasted into
the skin silencing the nightmares of a
generation we are not an x or twenty-
something
there is more to our teen spirit
it smells like distorted childhoods
and diapered friendships and parents
who fed us watergate and vietnam
and ronald reagan and saturday morning
cartoons without giving us a love we could
grip and suck on when the earth
was burning in our direction
and now you are gone
nah! i refuse to believe that
a whole bunch of us were gonna go and listen to you
regurgitate our blues (yours too) and make anxiety-
filled
guitar licks into a futuristic rock opera (our opera)
your hair would fly like a stringy flag saluting
the knuckleheads of the world,
yes! us! the post-civil rights post-vietnam post-reagan
babies would somehow feel validated when your
hoarse, garbled tongue
slapped the world with an indictment
that said
"you have neglected us for too long and look,

just look at what you have created"
and we would mosh and slam-dance, our bodies
contaminated with
this thing called youth, into a fitful overdose (isn't that
what they expect of us anyhow?)
of icon-worshipping you: but you are
alive!
tongue-kissing your feminine side on saturday night live
alive!
eating environmentally sound fruit next to river phoenix
and you whisper in james dean's ear
as janis, jimi, jim and john, the post-
happy days mount rushmore,
fall stone in love with the grunge thing
and someone will fanzine you
and call you a tragic genius
and bury you in mtv heaven
because no one no one no one
will ever understand why your flannel shirts
and ripped jeans and busted guitars mean
you have loved and lived much longer
than most of us...

she has many ancestors

for Lisa Teasley

confession:
i like artistic people who dabble in the predictable:
touch football, romances in paris, long-distance fondling
and none of the above.
perhaps.
should you be ashamed of who i am?
and i of you? nudity is nostalgic, beauty
buttresses the smile on your sepia frame. i dig
frames, especially if they encompass a picture
of dreadlocks jumping one, two, three over
a prayer with apples. in the garden the snakes
hiss at your ending, a beginning (for real) as the
accordion stretches a latin-flavored coda. tobacco juice
nibbles the crust off your day, fortified with a glass
of wine. do i detect a slight speech impediment?
express yourself before the boogie-wo/man
cross-references those wings

(Y)our mouth(s)

i'll be straightforward. happy
to receive your postmark 8/7, dated 7/30.
high top fades should converse. atlanta
eyes like hawks troopin' through a sewer
a moment, really, to plant and germinate
the harlem renaissance the black arts move
meant new voices old voices post-integration
blues kids but bomkauf isneverwas an
asterisk on my sole try earlyjonesginsbergkerouac
i dance nude on the front porch hiding is for
literaryfascists sippin' glue in academia
praytell what is a poem is poetry if it is not
a ballooned version of one's hairy butt cheeks?
ink is derivative (mine, i.e.) of hiphop standing
on the verge of a drumbeat the noise scares me
to death a special focus is tangible though
just shake the barbed wire from yo mouth.

Post-Bensonhurst Clues

At the moment when a people begin to realize a meaning *in their suffering, the civilization that engenders that suffering is doomed.*

— Richard Wright

9 is the fire sign
drip-drop jheri curl wearers
  and Rev. Al Sharpton
BEWARE
    your hairdos are out of style
i've got a hunch that will burn
right along the lines of demarcation
    of hostile territory

birds of a feather flocked together
    in jim's day
fortunately and unfortunately
    the alphabet organization pushed a mathematical concept
down the throats of unconscious solidarity

where is the steel helmet ralph ellison spoke of?
  history has made a sharp u-turn
        and is racing full speed
            backwards

the scenes have changed
the themes remain the same

come into our womb
and we will kill you
blind justice watches the backs
of perfect pawns inflicted with depraved difference
indifference?
no
difference
as in
i don't like you because you're different from me
(better yet)
it doesn't make a difference who you are
I HATE YOUR FUCKIN' GUTS!

sure someone got shot
no one saw it happen though
all mouths are shut tight with crazy glue
an entire community eternally up in arms
over hannibal's bad-ass hustle
into their native land

an elephant saw four mice
and panicked
three mice split
but the fourth couldn't find a hole

caught!
        crushed
                    blood
can we get a witness?
        oh wow
fama fled
        mondello maneuvered
yusef—
        he

                he be dead

usted senora.
habla ingles?
un poquito?
vio lo que paso?
usted lo vio?
porque usted no dijo nada ante?
porque se amenasaron.
ay dios mio! como usted se llama?
no hay problema, no es importante.
ayudenos por favor.
queremos libertad, justicia, E igualdad.

dick tracy
where are you?
we've got a clue hotter than madonna
the truth will make us all pee

who stole the soul of mayor david dinkins?
or was it a trade-off
for free teevee time and residence in gracie mansion?

if de mayor worked for george steinbrenner
he would have been fired four months ago
— brother
i'm scalping
brotherhood
sisterhood
and nationhood tickets
never mind i can't walk in your neighborhood
in the day-
time?
my watch stopped on April 4, 1968
burn baby burn!
i heard through the grapevine
that the beat(ings) will go on
'til the break of dawn
melts octopussy's oppressive oligarchy

damn
the gorgeous mosaic is the ugliest thing i've ever seen
and it smells like shit!

would someone please paint an accurate picture?
one that reflects injustice
hypocrisy
disease
one that reflects insanity
racism
death

one that reflects New York

Haiku #2

Yes, I need music.
The rhythms transcend my blues.
Why take that from me?

only children

the changes i've been going through
u kiss me that first time it shook
like a d.c. go-go dancer ancient yes
the emotion rolled back its sleeves
and dipped a man-child's pulse into
u i want(ed) to make love until sperm
& heat & u & me could reconcile our youth
the age of innocence manipulates youme but
u live with him i liked her and we kissed:
bodies undressing angerpainconfusion mary j.
blige moaning in the background 'bout two
only children playing with toys toying with
art & adulthood and we framed each other a
mirror skinned it really naked we finger &
nibble & lick the dust off our love and
we came so easily together to conclude that
this was suppose to be about friendship & not
love-making (evenifitdoesfeellliketheendofthe
worldandweareconnectedonafutondoingasixty-
nineyouowingmeowingyouanothertaste) unless it
means masturbating our souls coaxing a woman
& a man out of that pool of wetness

Soul Interlude

I.

i could have been billie holiday
dissecting that microphone
with a glass of cheap gin;
the blues come so easy
when the sky is embittered
from graffiti marks.
someone has etched the warning of george orwell:
remember the numbers, they must be
reversed
else time will have to teach itself to move

II.

a mouth is propelled by a language
i do not understand
the tongue
reddish-purple, bent at the gut
wags like a flag
saluting its neighbor

III.

it is a surrealistic longing:
to sleep inside the drunken head
of edgar allan poe
the tell-tale heart
ah yes,
it punches the floor
it bleeds irony
it sulks at my disobedience
it moons the sun

IV.

a spirit comes over me
s/he covers my dream
with an antiquated cobweb
i cannot move
but words fill the bowl of my throat
i want maternal protection
alas, my mother, she is gone—
the creases in her sheets
have finally captured her

harlem: neo-image

sunset nails the lip of a building:
a shadow eyes
            an ashy windowpane.
an old man sits on his cane
regurgitating cups of lenox
and the savoy:
i drink his face   it burps
southern clay and city welts

Southern Birth

for Lottie Bur(r)ison Powell
(February 23, 1912 - May 16, 1988)

a procession. southern wails. a yellow
face emerges specked with black moles.
two pennies slit the eyes where the dirt road
used to be. those thick glasses
distract from the tobacco-stained
teeth. tingling carolina stench braid
coarse charcoal hair.

i ache until it is wet, naked,
full of bounce: a gushing wind
corners a heart; puffy cotton veins
snap the way grandma lottie
broke string beans in the front yard.
a moist sound spills onto
the dirty plywood. reverend wilson's
eulogy fogs the church. homemade
syrup and cornbread descend. my mouth
plummets into an emotional abyss: a lover
flees the outhouse and a baby inherits the pain.

S.O.S.

for Howard Nisbeth

I.

bodies with vertical faces
blow an "A" train into the future.
note the bohemian artist:
romare bearden newsprints a hole on his thumbnail,
a coltrane riff dangles from his lips,
and the gods,
they hang him from a spiritual guidebook.

II.

below the sooty underground
we paint a poem of ghosts
bumping into eye sockets.
the eleventh hour gags the sun
and pours the moon into its back pocket;
desperation is a telephone call
where a voice mugs its echo.

III.

a bird, passing through concrete and deceit,
proclaims the transposition of time.
a nightmare postures as a daydream,
its brittle bones, like art,
an extension of a castrated desire.

& down again.
          butt-naked...
                    butt-naked...
          & living w/ 7 people
a sequel — for the strangers
colliding knee-caps
rigid, fossil-like, past
stories like the glory story
of a lovely lady...the youngest one in curls...

i could pretend the year was just
another teevee show, a mediocre sitcom
w/ a bedrock twist twist twist:
a brooklyn brownstone built on
layers of dynamite & class differences
(the colored artist's dilemma: am i petty bourgeois
or
a bourgie petty thief?)

nope. the real sitcoms cum as they are
burgundy liquid (that real sticky shit!)
drippin' from an itchy trigger finger
          as balloon-size lips mouth
"whassup dawg! you dead yet?"
& i pretend that east coast niggas
can understand the west coast tribe
but hands on the pumps make you wanna
jump! jump!
to a beat, like paul beatty,

scribble agitprop poetry that splatters
the acid trips of the cultural elite

(do we really care if they eat
unseasoned $12 hamburgers in beverly hills?)

& oh shit what am i doing there? one
nigga toad deposited into a charred existence
but rumor has it that punks jump up to get beat down
& learn to turn rhymes, drop dimes, and sip the hein'
lovetrap
hey, i luv u — the wind yes
she blows me off
(so much for a romance made in brooklyn)
and u saved me in a nick of time
watch those razor hickeys! shit!
& must we shave w/ him in the bathroom 2?

(i'm a lover; have always been; feel most comfortable
alone in a stadium full of screaming, foul-mouthed
beer cans)

it is so hard to breathe w/ a plastic nose
my nostrils here   pull the whiskers out...
the blood reminds me of the bell-bottoms &
black power afro picks:
feeling kinda retro

i want to make a triumphant return
to audubon park
play in the dark on the monkey bars
me and my cousin anthony
fall off
scrape knees
to collect baseball cards & stuff
them into my shop-rite truck
that george brett rookie card
reggie jackson as a yankee
(ah, the political possibilities of fragile youth!)

& the mudpies
me and anthony used to make mudpies
& eat 'em 2
bang! bang!
you dead
we killed each other before
b.m.p. (read: black male posturing)
was en vogue
& after grandpa pearley's casket yanked me into the world
unzipped
& you know i don't recall exactly when bob marley
swam into mister roger's neighborhood
it's a beautiful day to...get up stand up...
but it must've been around the same time

my
pubic hairs
descended into
a cave
&
i became a slave
2 da rhythm
knockin' the boots
off my wartime fantasies...

30 September 1991

for Tony Medina

tinted windows watch harlem nights
drive by
shooting crack vials at toothless stars
two young bards pen their imaginations
on the crisp, paper streets
where blood and urine jostle
for the salted flesh of st. nicholas ave.

between a plate of rice and beans
and musica salsa, a rat
cavorts on a garbage can, mesmerizing
a cardboard dreamwalker.
we shadow-box with paranoia:
ducking memories, we clench, then
jab the midnight hour

On Radcliffe Bailey

his name: Radcliffe Bailey, artist, twentysomething.
son of a son
who makes things with his hands. hand-me-
downs: ashe! dried flowers from an unmarked
grave. numbers and railroad spikes drive into the gut of
a painting — it flings tar and cotton; but

ogun has his back, the lord of the blacksmiths
smears bees wax along the edges of a
machete; like love, it protects the born
unnoticed. they love you love the rope-like
dreads the bushy goatee the bashfulness
he is *so* like and unlike basquiat! no, he is

like hip hop, a spin-off of his past, visually
collaged fragments & dreams & nightmares a
black past tormented by ax handles and guns
and hoses. he is a ladder climbing seven steps. his
grandfather made houses...bird
houses...he made things...he was an artist too...
no, they did not call him an artist but he was...
see the old family portraits: radcliffe might scratch
his name below and to the right of the portraits but

he might not. the portraits are always there. regal.
blank faces. black faces. blank black faces. all. most
anonymous. staring into the future: a spiritual migration
brushstroked
with tar. the tar babies are coming.
they pick the lint from
their church outfits they smooth out the wrinkles with
a branding iron they position themselves in the portraits
they,
like his art, are brown memories, tattered at the corners,
held captive by the times.

Twins

for Ni'Cole

one last cry for the lives we shed to be born. again
i feel your grandmother's touch a hand on the ceiling
(she's in the room...i know she is)
fanning a desire to be you
love you so much i
can't recall the death of my sins when i believed
life and love were evil twins stoning my bubble
dreams pop! that's the way love goes: a catchy
something for the radio hook the rhythms to your
heart i know you will be sincere forever, a colored
girl who knows this colored boy don't want no
suicide or fire this time we want it to be right
more than a wo/man we are two peas in a pod like
my ma used to say

recognize

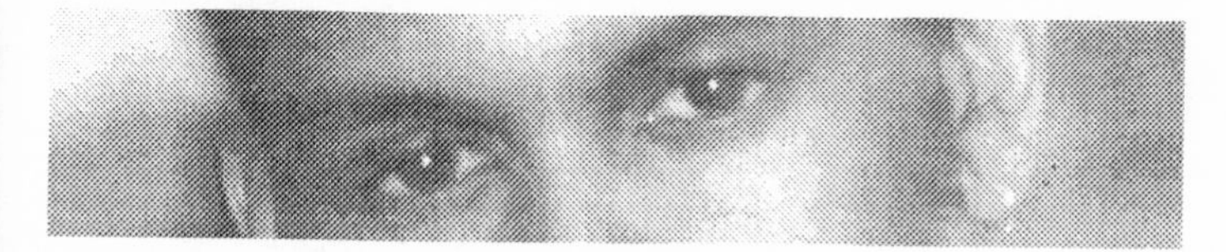

the evidence of things unseen
like my life
20/50 vision
blind-siding a poem with da dozen rhyme schemes:
yo' mama so black...she black!

we '90s nigs take mad rides on the hiphop side
& re-pre-sent! re-pre-sent!
hear the blackfolks
say it
1995
a number
another bummer
sounds like the funky drummer
done died
buried him ass-out
in 1994
the year
a carton of orange juice
monopolized the pulp fiction
and pulled
an alfred hitchcock on mister charlie's daughter

a slaughter?
you say

charlie manson is g-god
i mine-spray helter skelter
a homeless shelter
a ghetto dweller
a tittie sweller
nine inch nails pelted her
at lollapalooza
& woodstock
where the only niggas allowed
are the blunted lip hip homies with the skateboards,
jansport backpacks
and i-hate-white-people-but-i-really-want-to-be-down
bang-zoom poetics

but the extra point is i really can't boot
this identity crisis
thing

on side "A" a chapped-lip knuckle
with fake karl kani's and an
attitude straight outta the box
bumps me on fulton and flatbush
then says
"nigga, you *betta* recognize — you sleep you weep"
to which i responded
"ay-ight, it's your world"
to which he responded
"fuck the world nigga!"

then i figured
my problem was not him
but that i've been trying
to break north from the ghetto all my life
and forgot that star trek
—not the north star—
still runs in syndication

but real niggas don't run
they walk
like this
slo-mo stride
one leg bent for the flow
the other bent for the bounce
hands handcuffed to the front pockets
as they stone the temples &
pilot their way along flatbush ave

i was doin' my real nigga thang
one sunday
extra baggy levis draggin'
baseball cap strapped down like a helmet
when i saw the granite-face robots
ho-hummin' to a military beat
oh shit
do i cross the street and act like
i don't see them
or do i *walk on by*
and act like i know

fuck it! flatbush is for all the street benders

the robots got their swerve on good
tried to herb me
and gave me the one-two about t-h-e-m
da apocalypse now
& the rappin' prophet of rage
i wasn't wid biblical acrobatics so i kept steppin'

one of the robots said
you ain't real you ain't keepin' it real
my real middle finger went ballistic
and quicker than you could say
you confused mother—
it was on...

i could go on but you get my drift

side "B" goes a little something like this
niggas are in (again)
so let's get our loot on
and let 'em snatch crumbs
not dumb
i takes some
wear the mask (sometimes)
& play myself like a rubber band
i'm over here i'm over there
i'm super-nigga
my powerbook is the trigga

i figure
like chuck d said
when i get mad i put it down on a pad
but i never thought my pad would become a ball and
chain
suckin' up to the game

makes me wanna hol-ler a hymn
eternal father strong to save
& deliver me from the stone-age
where niggas and lies
— both of which do improvise —
think they rule
but cool-ass 2-bobs with peach-fuzz
and a 400-year itch for black ass
own the last hip hop
hooray
hey
ho
hey

and you don't stop

unless it leads you to therapy
for the third time in six years
hey, at least i'm batting .500
and the strike don't affect me
i pull into the bumper baby
and tell doctor so-and-so i'm steady trippin'

don't know who the fuck i am
    i wanna be down with that generation x thing
but everytime they talk about 18-30 year olds
they always seem to focus on the
    pale-face-existentialist-seeking-candy-apple-eating-
my-whole-body-is-pierced-
    i-take-ecstasy-on-sunset-boulevard-cocksucker
    who thinks vietnam and watergate
    and reagan and the recession are his/her/its modus
operandi
or
the reason why
  my own private idaho
    singles
      reality bites
and all the other cinematic capers
shadow-boxing with reality
are sooo fuckin' rad man

or even me
stupid kid that i was
thinking the real world would
make the real world safe
for ghetto-ology
but instead got branded
    bad boy entertainment
      way before puffy thought of the concept

we need *anger* kevin
yeah, oil the fire in your eyes
talk shit talk that racism shit
give us that ball scratchin' holy ghost emotion
you people are known for
Production Note #1: dutch-tilt camera three to catch the
spit
flooding the corners of his mouth
talk about your mother
how much you hate her
how black mothers make black sons hate them
talk about your father
never knew his dad motherfuck the...
okay, we'll take care of it in the edit room

it took me two and a half years to realize
life is one big edit room
just when you think you're done
someone off-lines another tape
and fucks up Act I
which lasts longer
than the crush america has on elvis

forever is the day i
listen to kind of blue
miles davis' horn palm-smackin'
my rib cage
sosososososo—-
so what

the music smells like a phillies blunt
hold it fold it roll it smoke it
takes me to back in the day when i was young
and a kid always and forever with a smile
talkin' 'bout
winstons' taste good just like a cigarette should
oosh ah i wanna piece of pie
the pie too sweet i wanna piece of meat
the meat too tough
hop on the bus
the bus too full
i wanna piece of bull
the bull too black
i want my money back
the money too green makes me mean
your father got a head like a tangerine

i loved those days when we settled beefs
toe-to-toe-elbow-to-elbow-crooked-afro-to-caesar-cut-with-
waves
at audubon park
thought jersey city — "chilltown j.c."
was the bomb
longed to fuck a white girl's brains out
float, float on...
and get down get down
pull your panties down
all i wanna do
is...

and we thought even the ugliest light-skinned hottie was
fine:
ain't nothin' in the world like a light-skinned girl
ain't nothin' in the sky that makes me fly so high...

yeah, pam grier was god with bullet-proof hips
& lips that could turn the nile river into a steam bath
"good times" was seeing black folks just like me
believin' that
a two-all-beef-patty-special-sauce-cheese-lettuce-tomato-
onions-on-a-sesame-seed-bun
was hot fun in the summertime
even while marvin gaye's tongue was slappin' fives
what's goin' on
45 records a warped soundtrack
for the afro picks smug affair with jheri curls
dancin'! dancin'! dancin'!
aaah freak out!

back then life was tackle football
on concrete
nigs using '76 novas
as the offensive line
some corny kid with high-waters and fake pro-keds
countin'
one mississippi two mississippi three mississippi...
'cuz us coool shorties had no patience for details

and i would dive for the football
the one that needed air in it but we used it anyway
'cuz nobody had an air pump
and i would pretend i was o.j.
or billie "white shoes" johnson
or tony dorsett
and twist and juke and dance in the end zone
bony black life contained inside chalk marks on the street

even the white kids knew we was smooth
they watched us play and believed black boys
were made of duncan hines mix with pecans on top
chocolate on the outside yellow on the inside
a cup of cherry kool-aid washing our shit down

inside the crib my other world came alive
i was john travolta
feel the city breakin' and everybody shakin'
stayin' alive stayin' alive
my camera the bathroom mirror
a big red jar of dax waving cream in one hand
hard-as-nails brush in the other
wondering how much of this stuff
i have to put in my hair to get it like *his* in *saturday night fever*

but i'm not a believer
anymore

hiphop was made for black boys who dreamed of suicide
when we discovered the rainbow wasn't enuf
a wicka-wicka-woom from the pot-belly of
post-integration blues people
you can't lose with the stuff we abuse
hiphop is about kickin' ass
    but no one told us on the way up it would take a
nation
        of soda cans to bacusdafucup

no doubt one day caged birds will wreck shop &
recognize
the price of the ticket is different if you
believe in dead presidents more than you
believe in your mamma
ma always said you make your bed
hard you sleep in it hard but she never
said nothin' about hard-ons
or cock-sneezin'
and catchin' that disease

now i recognize my wet dream was to dream
i have a dream
mlk said
and although i dig the man
i still can't picture this nig
cold-lampin' at the table with biff and susie
don't mean to be choosy

but if i can't bring morris, mook
and renaldo the hiphop junkie artist
guess who ain't comin' to dinner?

Kevin Powell is a staff writer at the New York-based *Vibe* magazine, a contributing editor to *Eyeball*, a literary arts journal, and co-editor of *In The Tradition: An Anthology of Young Black Writers*, with Ras Baraka. His memoir, *homeboy alone*, is forthcoming.

Other Writers and Readers books of poetry include:

Nova by Baron James Ashanti
Don't Explain by Alexis De Veaux
I Am a Black Woman by Mari Evans
A Dark & Splendid Mass by Mari Evans
Anointed to Fly by Gloria Wade Gayles
A Woman's Mourning Song by bell hooks
Daily Bread by Safiya Henderson-Holmes
Madness and a Bit of Hope by Safiya Henderson-Holmes
The Eye in the Ceiling by Eugene B. Redmond
Soft Song by Saundra Sharp
Typing in the Dark by Saundra Sharp
Weather Reports by Quincy Troupe